HIDE ME NOW!

My Internet and

Wi-Fi Passwords

notebook

OVERALL NOTES:

First things first:

Unless you are a single individual who also lives as a virtual recluse, you clearly don't want to leave this book in plain sight of visitors. Decide where you wish to hide this book where you will be able to find it but others will not (one suggestion is in your underwear drawer, underneath your fresh underwear). Once you've chosen a location, enter your password information on the pages provided.

Passwords that should never be used

While there are a number of recommendations for what makes for a strong password, there are also certain passwords that should never be used. Hackers routinely use computer generated attacks using many of the same commonly used passwords listed below when attempting identity theft. According to a recent CNET Magazine article, the top 25 passwords of all time, which are easily compromised and should never be used, are as follows:

123456
password
12345
12345678
qwerty
1234567890
1234
baseball
dragon
 football
1234567

monkey
letmein
abc123
111111
mustang
access
shadow
master
michael
superman
696969
123123
batman
trustno1

A strong password typically involves a combination of upper and lower-case letters, numbers, and non-alphanumeric characters such as the exclamation mark, underscore, or dollar signs. A password such as 'Mr3_51Bj12$!' is extremely difficult to compromise using the computer-generated attacks used by hackers.

Name

Web Address:

Login / User name:

Password:

Synchronized to?

Other remarks:

Name

Web Address:

Login / User name:

Password:

Synchronized to?

Other remarks:

Name

Web Address:

Login / User name:

Password:

Synchronized to?

Other remarks:

Name

Web Address:

Login / User name:

Password:

Synchronized to?

Other remarks:

Name

Web Address:

Login / User name:

Password:

Synchronized to?

Other remarks:

Name

Web Address:

Login / User name:

Password:

Synchronized to?

Other remarks:

Name

Web Address:

Login / User name:

Password:

Synchronized to?

Other remarks:

Name

Web Address:

Login / User name:

Password:

Synchronized to?

Other remarks:

D

Name

Web Address:

Login / User name:

Password:

Synchronized to?

Other remarks:

Name

Web Address:

Login / User name:

Password:

Synchronized to?

Other remarks:

Name

Web Address:

Login / User name:

Password:

Synchronized to?

Other remarks:

Name

Web Address:

Login / User name:

Password:

Synchronized to?

Other remarks:

Name

Web Address:

Login / User name:

Password:

Synchronized to?

Other remarks:

Name

Web Address:

Login / User name:

Password:

Synchronized to?

Other remarks:

Name

Web Address:

Login / User name:

Password:

Synchronized to?

Other remarks:

Name

Web Address:

Login / User name:

Password:

Synchronized to?

Other remarks:

Name
_____

Web Address:
_____

Login / User name:
_____

Password:
_____

Synchronized to?
_____

Other remarks:
_____

Name
_____

Web Address:
_____

Login / User name:
_____

Password:
_____

Synchronized to?
_____

Other remarks:
_____

Name
_____

Web Address:
_____

Login / User name:
_____

Password:
_____

Synchronized to?
_____

Other remarks:
_____

Name
_____

Web Address:
_____

Login / User name:
_____

Password:
_____

Synchronized to?
_____

Other remarks:
_____

Name
_____

Web Address:
_____

Login / User name:
_____

Password:
_____

Synchronized to?
_____

Other remarks:
_____

Name
_____

Web Address:
_____

Login / User name:
_____

Password:
_____

Synchronized to?
_____

Other remarks:
_____

Name
_____

Web Address:
_____

Login / User name:
_____

Password:
_____

Synchronized to?
_____

Other remarks:
_____

Name
_____

Web Address:
_____

Login / User name:
_____

Password:
_____

Synchronized to?
_____

Other remarks:
_____

Name
_____

Web Address:
_____

Login / User name:
_____

Password:*
_____

Synchronized to?
_____

Other remarks:
_____

Name
_____

Web Address:
_____

Login / User name:
_____

Password:
_____

Synchronized to?
_____

Other remarks:
_____

Name
_____

Web Address:
_____

Login / User name:
_____

Password:
_____

Synchronized to?
_____

Other remarks:
_____

Name
_____

Web Address:
_____

Login / User name:
_____

Password:
_____

Synchronized to?
_____

Other remarks:
_____

/

Name

Web Address:

Login / User name:

Password:

Synchronized to?

Other remarks:

Name

Web Address:

Login / User name:

Password:

Synchronized to?

Other remarks:

Name

Web Address:

Login / User name:

Password:

Synchronized to?

Other remarks:

Name

Web Address:

Login / User name:

Password:

Synchronized to?

Other remarks:

Name

Web Address:

Login / User name:

Password:

Synchronized to?

Other remarks:

Name

Web Address:

Login / User name:

Password:

Synchronized to?

Other remarks:

Name

Web Address:

Login / User name:

Password:

Synchronized to?

Other remarks:

Name

Web Address:

Login / User name:

Password:

Synchronized to?

Other remarks:

Name
_____

Web Address:
_____

Login / User name:
_____

Password:
_____

Synchronized to?
_____

Other remarks:
_____

Name
_____

Web Address:
_____

Login / User name:
_____

Password:
_____

Synchronized to?
_____

Other remarks:
_____

Name
_____

Web Address:
_____

Login / User name:
_____

Password:
_____

Synchronized to?
_____

Other remarks:
_____

Name
_____

Web Address:
_____

Login / User name:
_____

Password:
_____

Synchronized to?
_____

Other remarks:
_____

H

Name

Web Address:

Login / User name:

Password:

Synchronized to?

Other remarks:

Name

Web Address:

Login / User name:

Password:

Synchronized to?

Other remarks:

Name

Web Address:

Login / User name:

Password:

Synchronized to?

Other remarks:

Name

Web Address:

Login / User name:

Password:

Synchronized to?

Other remarks:

Name
_____

Web Address:
_____

Login / User name:
_____

Password:
_____

Synchronized to?
_____

Other remarks:
_____

Name
_____

Web Address:
_____

Login / User name:
_____

Password:
_____

Synchronized to?
_____

Other remarks:
_____

Name
_____

Web Address:
_____

Login / User name:
_____

Password:
_____

Synchronized to?
_____

Other remarks:
_____

Name
_____

Web Address:
_____

Login / User name:
_____

Password:
_____

Synchronized to?
_____

Other remarks:

Name

_____

Web Address:

_____

Login / User name:

_____

Password:

_____

Synchronized to?

_____

Other remarks:

_____

Name

_____

Web Address:

_____

Login / User name:

_____

Password:

_____

Synchronized to?

_____

Other remarks:

_____

Name

_____

Web Address:

_____

Login / User name:

_____

Password:

_____

Synchronized to?

_____

Other remarks:

_____

Name

_____

Web Address:

_____

Login / User name:

_____

Password:

_____

Synchronized to?

_____

Other remarks:

_____

Name

_____

Web Address:

_____

Login / User name:

_____

Password:

_____

Synchronized to?

_____

Other remarks:

_____

Name

_____

Web Address:

_____

Login / User name:

_____

Password:

_____

Synchronized to?

_____

Other remarks:

_____

Name

_____

Web Address:

_____

Login / User name:

_____

Password:

_____

Synchronized to?

_____

Other remarks:

_____

Name

_____

Web Address:

_____

Login / User name:

_____

Password:

_____

Synchronized to?

_____

Other remarks:

_____

Name

Web Address:

Login / User name:

Password:

Synchronized to?

Other remarks:

Name

Web Address:

Login / User name:

Password:

Synchronized to?

Other remarks:

Name

Web Address:

Login / User name:

Password:

Synchronized to?

Other remarks:

Name

Web Address:

Login / User name:

Password:

Synchronized to?

Other remarks:

Name

Web Address:

Login / User name:

Password:

Synchronized to?

Other remarks:

Name

Web Address:

Login / User name:

Password:

Synchronized to?

Other remarks:

Name

Web Address:

Login / User name:

Password:

Synchronized to?

Other remarks:

Name

Web Address:

Login / User name:

Password:

Synchronized to?

Other remarks:

Name

Web Address:

Login / User name:

Password:

Synchronized to?

Other remarks:

Name

Web Address:

Login / User name:

Password:

Synchronized to?

Other remarks:

Name

Web Address:

Login / User name:

Password:

Synchronized to?

Other remarks:

Name

Web Address:

Login / User name:

Password:

Synchronized to?

Other remarks:

Name
_____

Web Address:
_____

Login / User name:
_____

Password:
_____

Synchronized to?
_____

Other remarks:
_____

Name
_____

Web Address:
_____

Login / User name:
_____

Password:
_____

Synchronized to?
_____

Other remarks:
_____

Name
_____

Web Address:
_____

Login / User name:
_____

Password:
_____

Synchronized to?
_____

Other remarks:
_____

Name
_____

Web Addess:
_____

Login / User name:
_____

Password:
_____

Synchronized to?
_____

Other remarks:
_____

L

Name
_____
Web Address:
_____
Login / User name:
_____
Password:
_____
Synchronized to?
_____
Other remarks:
_____

Name
_____
Web Address:
_____
Login / User name:
_____
Password:
_____
Synchronized to?
_____
Other remarks:
_____

Name
_____
Web Address:
_____
Login / User name:
_____
Password:
_____
Synchronized to?
_____
Other remarks:
_____

Name
_____
Web Address:
_____
Login / User name:
_____
Password:
_____
Synchronized to?
_____
Other remarks:
_____

Name

Web Address:

Login / User name:

Password:

Synchronized to?

Other remarks:

Name

Web Address:

Login / User name:

Password:

Synchronized to?

Other remarks:

Name

Web Address:

Login / User name:

Password:

Synchronized to?

Other remarks:

Name

Web Address:

Login / User name:

Password:

Synchronized to?

Other remarks:

Name

Web Address:

Login / User name:

Password:

Synchronized to?

Other remarks:

Name

Web Address:

Login / User name:

Password:

Synchronized to?

Other remarks:

Name

Web Address:

Login / User name:

Password:

Synchronized to?

Other remarks:

Name

Web Address:

Login / User name:

Password:

Synchronized to?

Other remarks:

Name
_____
Web Address:
_____
Login / User name:
_____
Password:
_____
Synchronized to?
_____
Other remarks:
_____

Name
_____
Web Address:
_____
Login / User name:
_____
Password:
_____
Synchronized to?
_____
Other remarks:
_____

Name
_____
Web Address:
_____
Login / User name:
_____
Password:
_____
Synchronized to?
_____
Other remarks:
_____

Name
_____
Web Address:
_____
Login / User name:
_____
Password:
_____
Synchronized to?
_____
Other remarks:
_____

Name

Web Address:

Login / User name:

Password:*

Synchronized to?

Other remarks:

Name

Web Address:

Login / User name:

Password:

Synchronized to?

Other remarks:

Name

Web Address:

Login / User name:

Password:

Synchronized to?

Other remarks:

Name

Web Address:

Login / User name:

Password:

Synchronized to?

Other remarks:

/

Name

Web Address:

Login / User name:

Password:

Synchronized to?

Other remarks:

Name

Web Address:

Login / User name:

Password:

Synchronized to?

Other remarks:

Name

Web Address:

Login / User name:

Password:

Synchronized to?

Other remarks:

Name

Web Address:

Login / User name:

Password:

Synchronized to?

Other remarks:

Name
_____

Web Address:
_____

Login / User name:
_____

Password:
_____

Synchronized to?
_____

Other remarks:
_____

Name
_____

Web Address:
_____

Login / User name:
_____

Password:
_____

Synchronized to?
_____

Other remarks:
_____

Name
_____

Web Address:
_____

Login / User name:
_____

Password:
_____

Synchronized to?
_____

Other remarks:
_____

Name
_____

Web Address:
_____

Login / User name:
_____

Password:
_____

Synchronized to?
_____

Other remarks:
_____

Name

Web Address:

Login / User name:

Password:

Synchronized to?

Other remarks:

Name

Web Address:

Login / User name:

Password:

Synchronized to?

Other remarks:

Name

Web Address:

Login / User name:

Password:

Synchronized to?

Other remarks:

Name

Web Address:

Login / User name:

Password:

Synchronized to?

Other remarks:

Name

Web Address:

Login / User name:

Password:

Synchronized to?

Other remarks:

Name

Web Address:

Login / User name:

Password:

Synchronized to?

Other remarks:

Name

Web Address:

Login / User name:

Password:

Synchronized to?

Other remarks:

Name

Web Address:

Login / User name:

Password:

Synchronized to?

Other remarks:

Name

Web Address:

Login / User name:

Password:

Synchronized to?

Other remarks:

Name

Web Address:

Login / User name:

Password:

Synchronized to?

Other remarks:

Name

Web Address:

Login / User name:

Password:

Synchronized to?

Other remarks:

Name

Web Address:

Login / User name:

Password:

Synchronized to?

Other remarks:

Name

Web Address:

Login / User name:

Password:

Synchronized to?

Other remarks:

Name

Web Address:

Login / User name:

Password:

Synchronized to?

Other remarks:

Name

Web Address:

Login / User name:

Password:

Synchronized to?

Other remarks:

Name

Web Address:

Login / User name:

Password:

Synchronized to?

Other remarks:

Name

Web Address:

Login / User name:

Password:

Synchronized to?

Other remarks:

Name

Web Address:

Login / User name:

Password:

Synchronized to?

Other remarks:

Name

Web Address:

Login / User name:

Password:

Synchronized to?

Other remarks:

Name

Web Address:

Login / User name:

Password:

Synchronized to?

Other remarks:

R

Name
_____

Web Address:
_____

Login / User name:
_____

Password:
_____

Synchronized to?
_____

Other remarks:
_____

Name
_____

Web Address:
_____

Login / User name:
_____

Password:
_____

Synchronized to?
_____

Other remarks:
_____

Name
_____

Web Address:
_____

Login / User name:
_____

Password:
_____

Synchronized to?
_____

Other remarks:
_____

Name
_____

Web Address:
_____

Login / User name:
_____

Password:
_____

Synchronized to?
_____

Other remarks:
_____

Name

Web Address:

Login / User name:

Password:

Synchronized to?

Other remarks:

Name

Web Address:

Login / User name:

Password:

Synchronized to?

Other remarks:

Name

Web Address:

Login / User name:

Password:

Synchronized to?

Other remarks:

Name

Web Address:

Login / User name:

Password:

Synchronized to?

Other remarks:

Name

Web Address:

Login / User name:

Password:

Synchronized to?

Other remarks:

Name

Web Address:

Login / User name:

Password:

Synchronized to?

Other remarks:

Name

Web Address:

Login / User name:

Password:

Synchronized to?

Other remarks:

Name

Web Address:

Login / User name:

Password:

Synchronized to?

Other remarks:

Name

_____

Web Address:

_____

Login / User name:

_____

Password:

_____

Synchronized to?

_____

Other remarks:

_____

Name

_____

Web Address:

_____

Login / User name:

_____

Password:

_____

Synchronized to?

_____

Other remarks:

_____

Name

_____

Web Address:

_____

Login / User name:

_____

Password:

_____

Synchronized to?

_____

Other remarks:

_____

Name

_____

Web Address:

_____

Login / User name:

_____

Password:

_____

Synchronized to?

_____

Other remarks:

_____

Name

Web Address:

Login / User name:

Password:

Synchronized to?

Other remarks:

Name

Web Address:

Login / User name:

Password:

Synchronized to?

Other remarks:

Name

Web Address:

Login / User name:

Password:

Synchronized to?

Other remarks:

Name

Web Address:

Login / User name:

Password:

Synchronized to?

Other remarks:

Name

Web Address:

Login / User name:

Password:

Synchronized to?

Other remarks:

Name

Web Address:

Login / User name:

Password:

Synchronized to?

Other remarks:

Name

Web Address:

Login / User name:

Password:

Synchronized to?

Other remarks:

Name

Web Address:

Login / User name:

Password:

Synchronized to?

Other remarks:

Name
_____

Web Address:
_____

Login / User name:
_____

Password:
_____

Synchronized to?
_____

Other remarks:
_____

Name
_____

Web Address:
_____

Login / User name:
_____

Password:
_____

Synchronized to?
_____

Other remarks:
_____

Name
_____

Web Address:
_____

Login / User name:
_____

Password:
_____

Synchronized to?
_____

Other remarks:
_____

Name
_____

Web Address:
_____

Login / User name:
_____

Password:
_____

Synchronized to?
_____

Other remarks:
_____

Name

Web Address:

Login / User name:

Password:

Synchronized to?

Other remarks:

Name

Web Address:

Login / User name:

Password:

Synchronized to?

Other remarks:

Name

Web Address:

Login / User name:

Password:

Synchronized to?

Other remarks:

Name

Web Address:

Login / User name:

Password:

Synchronized to?

Other remarks:

V

Name
_____

Web Address:
_____

Login / User name:
_____

Password:*
_____

Synchronized to?
_____

Other remarks:
_____

Name
_____

Web Address:
_____

Login / User name:
_____

Password:
_____

Synchronized to?
_____

Other remarks:
_____

Name
_____

Web Address:
_____

Login / User name:
_____

Password:
_____

Synchronized to?
_____

Other remarks:
_____

Name
_____

Web Address:
_____

Login / User name:
_____

Password:
_____

Synchronized to?
_____

Other remarks:
_____

/

Name

Web Address:

Login / User name:

Password:

Synchronized to?

Other remarks:

Name

Web Address:

Login / User name:

Password:

Synchronized to?

Other remarks:

Name

Web Address:

Login / User name:

Password:

Synchronized to?

Other remarks:

Name

Web Address:

Login / User name:

Password:

Synchronized to?

Other remarks:

W

Name
_____

Web Address:
_____

Login / User name:
_____

Password:
_____

Synchronized to?
_____

Other remarks:
_____

Name
_____

Web Address:
_____

Login / User name:
_____

Password:
_____

Synchronized to?
_____

Other remarks:
_____

Name
_____

Web Address:
_____

Login / User name:
_____

Password:
_____

Synchronized to?
_____

Other remarks:
_____

Name
_____

Web Address:
_____

Login / User name:
_____

Password:
_____

Synchronized to?
_____

Other remarks:
_____

Name

Web Address:

Login / User name:

Password:

Synchronized to?

Other remarks:

Name

Web Address:

Login / User name:

Password:

Synchronized to?

Other remarks:

Name

Web Address:

Login / User name:

Password:

Synchronized to?

Other remarks:

Name

Web Address:

Login / User name:

Password:

Synchronized to?

Other remarks:

X

Name
_____

Web Address:
_____

Login / User name:
_____

Password:
_____

Synchronized to?
_____

Other remarks:
_____

Name
_____

Web Address:
_____

Login / User name:
_____

Password:
_____

Synchronized to?
_____

Other remarks:
_____

Name
_____

Web Address:
_____

Login / User name:
_____

Password:
_____

Synchronized to?
_____

Other remarks:
_____

Name
_____

Web Address:
_____

Login / User name:
_____

Password:
_____

Synchronized to?
_____

Other remarks:
_____

Name
_____

Web Address:
_____

Login / User name:
_____

Password:
_____

Synchronized to?
_____

Other remarks:
_____

Name
_____

Web Address:
_____

Login / User name:
_____

Password:
_____

Synchronized to?
_____

Other remarks:
_____

Name
_____

Web Address:
_____

Login / User name:
_____

Password:
_____

Synchronized to?
_____

Other remarks:
_____

Name
_____

Web Address:
_____

Login / User name:
_____

Password:
_____

Synchronized to?
_____

Other remarks:

Name

Web Address:

Login / User name:

Password:

Synchronized to?

Other remarks:

Name

Web Address:

Login / User name:

Password:

Synchronized to?

Other remarks:

Name

Web Address:

Login / User name:

Password:

Synchronized to?

Other remarks:

Name

Web Address:

Login / User name:

Password:

Synchronized to?

Other remarks:

Name

Web Address:

Login / User name:

Password:

Synchronized to?

Other remarks:

Name

Web Address:

Login / User name:

Password:

Synchronized to?

Other remarks:

Name

Web Address:

Login / User name:

Password:

Synchronized to?

Other remarks:

Name

Web Address:

Login / User name:

Password:

Synchronized to?

Other remarks:

Z

Name
_____

Web Address:
_____

Login / User name:
_____

Password:
_____

Synchronized to?
_____

Other remarks:
_____

Name
_____

Web Address:
_____

Login / User name:
_____

Password:
_____

Synchronized to?
_____

Other remarks:
_____

Name
_____

Web Address:
_____

Login / User name:
_____

Password:
_____

Synchronized to?
_____

Other remarks:
_____

Name
_____

Web Address:
_____

Login / User name:
_____

Password:
_____

Synchronized to?
_____

Other remarks:
_____

Name
_____

Web Address:
_____

Login / User name:
_____

Password:
_____

Synchronized to?
_____

Other remarks:
_____

Name
_____

Web Address:
_____

Login / User name:
_____

Password:
_____

Synchronized to?
_____

Other remarks:
_____

Name
_____

Web Address:
_____

Login / User name:
_____

Password:
_____

Synchronized to?
_____

Other remarks:
_____

Name
_____

Web Address:
_____

Login / User name:
_____

Password:
_____

Synchronized to?
_____

Other remarks:
_____

Name

Web Address:

Login / User name:

Password:

Synchronized to?

Other remarks:

Name

Web Address:

Login / User name:

Password:

Synchronized to?

Other remarks:

Name

Web Address:

Login / User name:

Password:

Synchronized to?

Other remarks:

Name

Web Address:

Login / User name:

Password:

Synchronized to?

Other remarks:

Name

Web Address:

Login / User name:

Password:

Synchronized to?

Other remarks:

Name

Web Address:

Login / User name:

Password:

Synchronized to?

Other remarks:

Name

Web Address:

Login / User name:

Password:

Synchronized to?

Other remarks:

Name

Web Address:

Login / User name:

Password:

Synchronized to?

Other remarks:

Name

Web Address:

Login / User name:

Password:

Synchronized to?

Other remarks:

Name

Web Address:

Login / User name:

Password:

Synchronized to?

Other remarks:

Name

Web Address:

Login / User name:

Password:

Synchronized to?

Other remarks:

Name

Web Address:

Login / User name:

Password:

Synchronized to?

Other remarks:

Name

Web Address:

Login / User name:

Password:

Synchronized to?

Other remarks:

Name

Web Address:

Login / User name:

Password:

Synchronized to?

Other remarks:

Name

Web Address:

Login / User name:

Password:

Synchronized to?

Other remarks:

Name

Web Address:

Login / User name:

Password:

Synchronized to?

Other remarks:

Name

Web Address:

Login / User name:

Password:*

Synchronized to?

Other remarks:

Name

Web Address:

Login / User name:

Password:

Synchronized to?

Other remarks:

Name

Web Address:

Login / User name:

Password:

Synchronized to?

Other remarks:

Name

Web Address:

Login / User name:

Password:

Synchronized to?

Other remarks:

/

Name

Web Address:

Login / User name:

Password:

Synchronized to?

Other remarks:

Name

Web Address:

Login / User name:

Password:

Synchronized to?

Other remarks:

Name

Web Address:

Login / User name:

Password:

Synchronized to?

Other remarks:

Name

Web Address:

Login / User name:

Password:

Synchronized to?

Other remarks:

INTERNET and WIRELESS NETWORK INFORMATION

Internet provider: _____

Wireless network password: _____

(This can often be found on a label on the underside of your cable or phone company's internet modem.)

Customer service phone: _____

Technical support phone: _____

COMMON PROVIDER SUPPORT NUMBERS

ATT U-Verse Internet	1 800 288-2020
Charter Communications	1 888 438-2427
Comcast / Xfinity	1 800 XFINITY
Cox Communications	1 877 832-7658
Earthlink	1 888 327-8454
Time Warner Cable	1 800 892-4357
Verizon FIOS	1 800 837-4966
Windstream Communications	1 866 445-3194

Additional Notes

My Tablets and Cellphone Logins

Device Name: _____

Login password: _____

Device Name: _____

Login password: _____

Device Name: _____

Login password: _____

Device Name: _____

Login password: _____

HIDE ME NOW!

My Internet and Wi-Fi passwords notebook

Edward Jones

www.ingramcontent.com/pod-product-compliance
Lightning Source LLC
Chambersburg PA
CBHW060502060326
40689CB00020B/4605